REMEDIES

BY ANNI

ILLUSTRATIONS BY NINA RIPICH
FILM BY MIRA HORWITZ

Dedicated to my mother, who believed words could heal. Who
encouraged me to write everything down.
Who framed the first poem I wrote and hung it on a wall. Who
inspired me every day of her life, to love without fear, to be
vulnerable in your art,
let things go, let things flow, and fill your life with passion.

May these words heal.
May these poems be remedies.

For after every fire, the wildflowers
bloom brighter than before.
The earth rebirths and grows again.
And we do too.

You said ˙I think my purpose is to find the beauty here˙
The beauty in every person you meet
Whether they be a season or a lifetime
Remember winter comes and so does spring
Flowers bloom accordingly
The beauty in love
Romantic and Platonic
How it engulfs us
And how it astounds us
The beauty in kindness
From a stranger to a friend
the touch of one another
Without skin
The beauty that comes from within
You found the beauty in everything
You really truly did
I think my purpose in this life
Is to find the beauty
In hopes
As much as you did.

LOVE

Remedy for when you love someone

Sage is used for rebirth and cleansing. Smudging
can be a powerful ritual that purifies the space and
removes negative energy. It is used for clearing and
protection. When starting a chapter with someone, clear
the negativity from the past, and start anew in the
present.

I want to have a love
that lasts beneath our skin
lives within bones
and protects when broken
runs through veins
and has more intention than touch

I was told to fall in love more.
I love the marine layer in the morning
The spots of fog over the buildings
I love Autumn
And the pale leaves
Before everything goes to sleep
I love my mom's activism
My dad's happy tears
Rare and oh so dear
I love Mia's long stories
Every detail
And the way Sofia laughs with her whole body
I love Bethany's kindness
And Jill's perseverance
I love the baristas eyes
And the check out counter lady's kindness
I love my neighbors shouts of joy at the game on T.V.
And the gardeners optimism
I love Nellie's hugs
And Keira's head rubs
I love morning sand in summer
Soft and untouched
And the cold weather days under covers
You and I's blanket tug of wars
Lazy Sundays
Calm before the storms

Remedies

What is a mother

A mother is a presence
A mother is a person
A mother is a guardian angel
A mother is a stable
Where a horse can roam
And always come home
A mother is who births you
But can also be who chooses you
A mother is a hand taken
A shoulder for support
A life line or prayer
A mother can come in many shapes and sizes
Physical or soul
But a mother surrounds you
No matter where you roam
A mother is a stable
Even the wild horses can call home

I long for the days
When I was little
and the only worry was
What am I going to wear to school tomorrow?
And if my crush knows I like him
or not
And if they'd have pesto pasta for lunch
in the cafe
or just that shitty salad bar
And if the letters A+J that I carved into
'the log' on the playground with my pen
with the squishy gripper was noticeable
I guess it was
Because my next worry was
After he saw it
How was I going to explain
That caterpillars are breaking out of their cocoons
In my stomach
Every time
I look at you

-First love

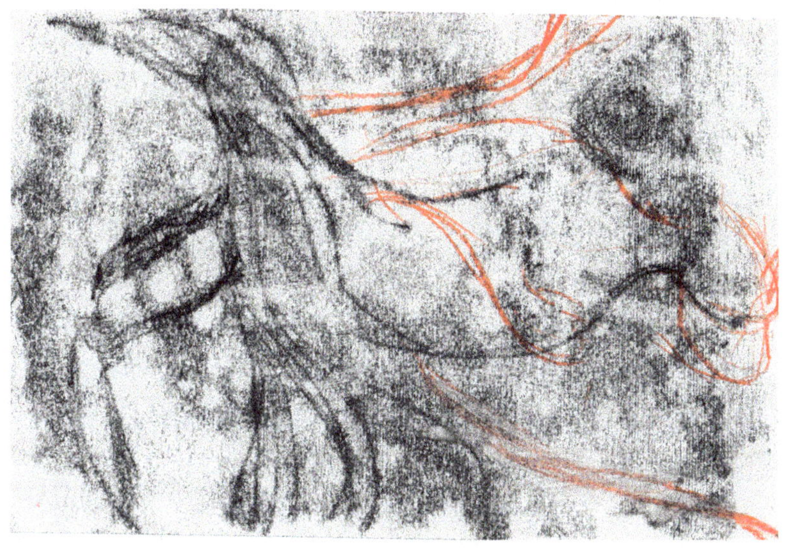

My mother saw hearts
in everything
She'd collect all the love shaped things
All the rocks, and wood, crystals and leaves
and leave them scattered across the house
On her jewelry stand
By her bed
In her car
In her purse
She'd give them as gifts
and when she ran out
She'd run back to the beach
I started doing the same thing
and noticed
heart shaped rocks aren't easy
to find in a sea of sand
But somehow she managed
to bring one home
each time
and place it in my hand

For she saw love
in everything
It must have been so beautiful
to see the world
through her eyes
one heart rock at a time

You deserve someone who sits atop a moon for you
Who hands you stars on your dark days
Who carries the sun when you need warmth
You deserve someone who sees your imperfections
And still calls them beautiful
Who knows your worth
Your uniqueness
And thinks how lucky they are to be next to you
For there is only one you
You deserve someone's absolute
Not to be someone's maybe
You deserve someone to walk with
Not follow
Or persuade
Someone to succeed together with
Challenge
Ignite
For where there is a shooting star
Its luck to see more than one
In a single night
You deserve to be loved
And to love someone
Just as bright

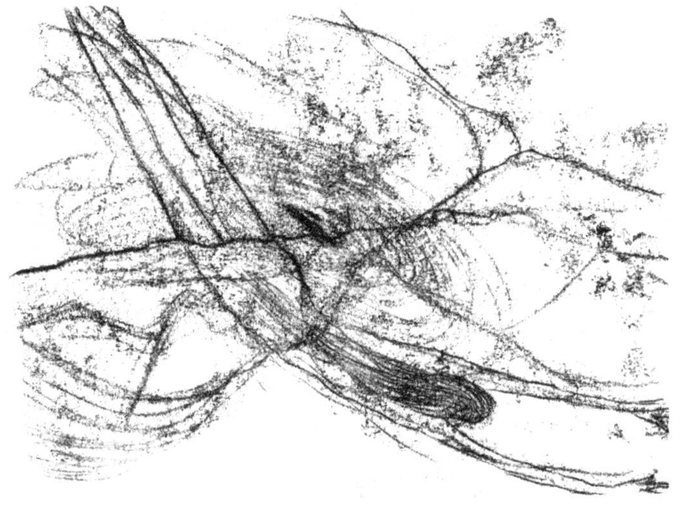

I'm beginning to love this city
The quiet that surrounds you in a late night taxi home
The rumble of the cobble stone streets under its wheels
I feel the presence of excitement
Tingle through the gum stained concrete
And the buzz of peoples voices
Through the open apartment windows
I'm beginning to love this city
Even though it can sometimes be hard to love
But the heels will continue to click the pavement
Like fingers to a keyboard
And the homeless man will shout his name
With a Broadway appeal
The sun will set on each building
One by one by one
Engulfing slowly each brick into a fiery light

I'm learning to love
Less in black and white
But in water color
In a vivid
Amalgamation of blues and yellows and reds
Wading in water of gray
Complimentary
Of each other's strokes and blends
And puddles
Of colors we will never be able to comprehend
But we make a beautiful canvas
In the end

You make the freckles on my back dance with anticipation
You make my lungs against my spine
Inhale
Exhale
Quickly
In time with my heartbeat
You make the hairs on my arm stick up
Prickly
and you make my lips tingle
at the touch of yours on my cheek
You make my eyes smile
and my teeth twinkle
You make my feelings fast but my actions slow
if only you could know

A tranquil lullaby
To my livened thirst
A grassy patch
in place of gravel dirt
An eye for an eye
More beautiful than I
could ever imagine
A monarch in spring
when it's still brisk to the bone
But you smile
and say
Let me take you home

You hold me like a river
You let me run
You let me flow
You let me ripple
You let me...
Waterfall

A tangled mess
of scruff against spine
Lips against shoulder
Hands drawing infinity signs
Across growling bellies
Hearts against hands
Limbs on top of limbs
Like fallen tree trunks
Feet against white sheets
Fingers against curly hair
Lions mane at its best
Early in the morning
Chest against chest
Forehead against forehead
Breast against breast
We were a beautiful mess
of skin
Color
Texture
Tangled beneath those four walls

She let her lips
Take another sip
as he spoke
of all his pretty problems
Pretty because each one
Made her love him
Even more
Each scar
He let her see
Made her strip a little more

You're imperfectly perfect
With flaws no one can see
Your smile is one of a young child
and your teeth and tongue agree
Your eyes are indents
to your soul underneath
and your jawline
is a map to
Where I want to be

Remedies

Our love is a compilation of
pit stop gas stations
abandoned homes
and RVs
along the highway
Our love is the road between the city
and the mountains
the snow and the desert
the patches of clouds
against the hillsides
Our love is in
a subway sandwich
and road trip playlists
and car mileages
Our love is a collection
of gas receipts
and cold soda
of street signs
And the vast
open road
of the California desert

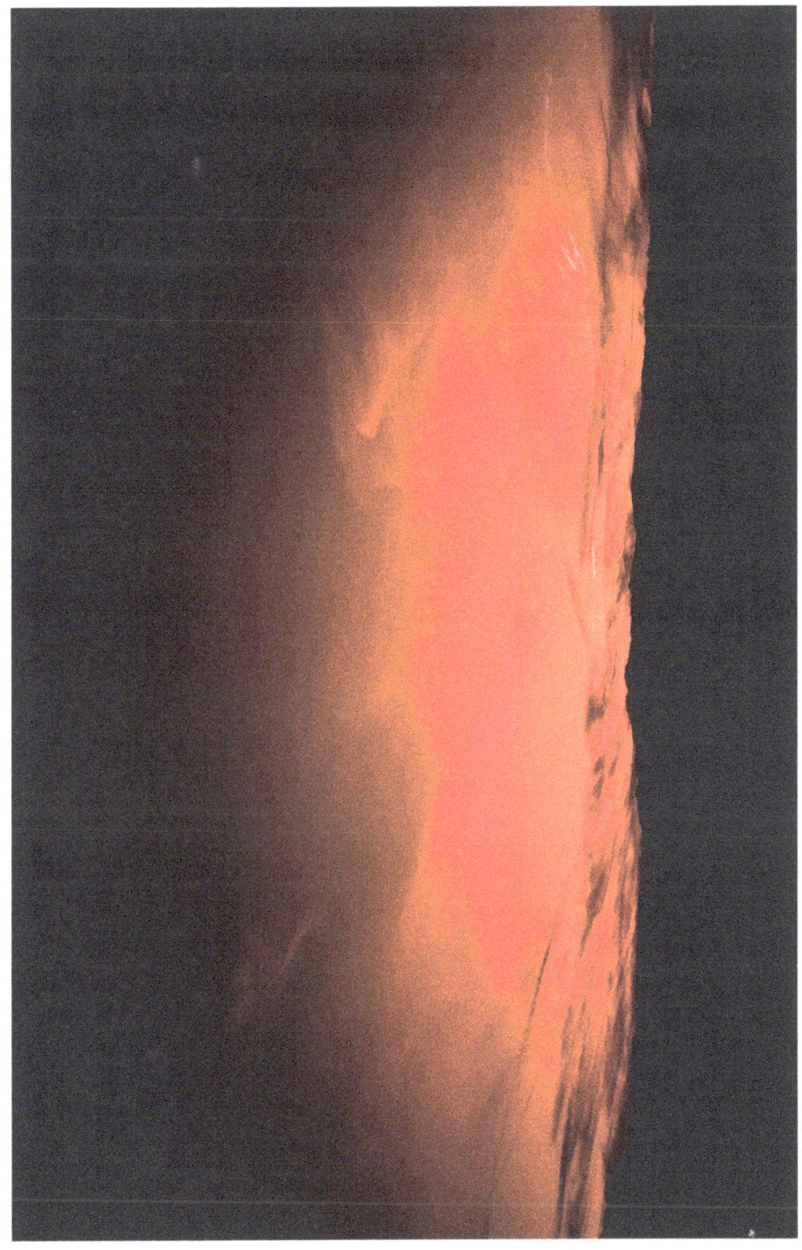

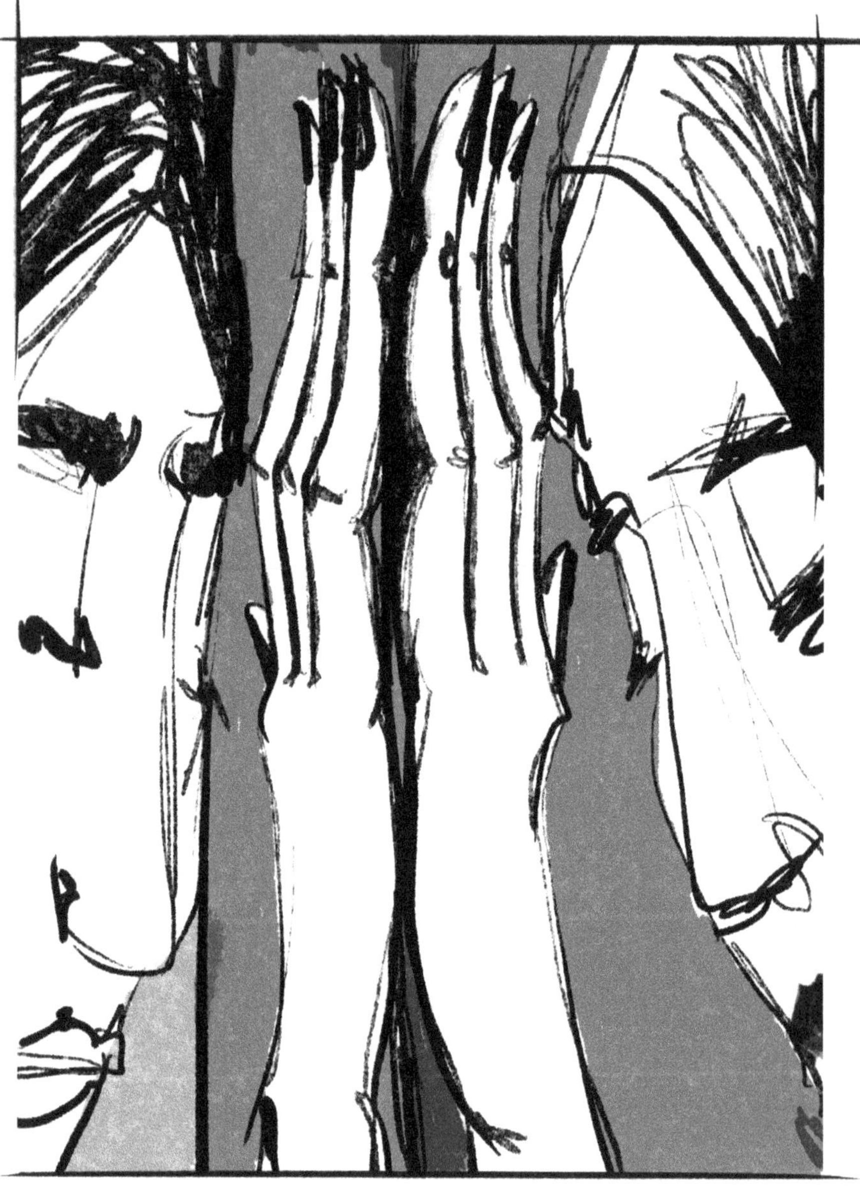

I would only hope

to be a mother

like mine

to a daughter

To grow her up

with morals and memories

with food that truly feeds my soul

Hands that will always brush my hair

and lessons on when I need to stand tall

Activism at is best and a real force of power

Strength yet softness

of calm but yet controlled

My mother sewn kindness

into my skin

Words of wisdom

down my throat

and love through my veins

She bore light

when I was dark

and confidence

when I was not at my best

She's a mirror

of who I want

ought

to be

And I strongly believe

if every woman had a mother like her

There would be a lot more goodness

and grace

I can only hope

to be a mother

like mine

Love doesn't always have to break you
What happened in the past
won't repeat itself
unless you let it
Patterns repeat but break when realized
Love doesn't have to be the way you've seen it played out
Love
won't always break you
But maybe make you better

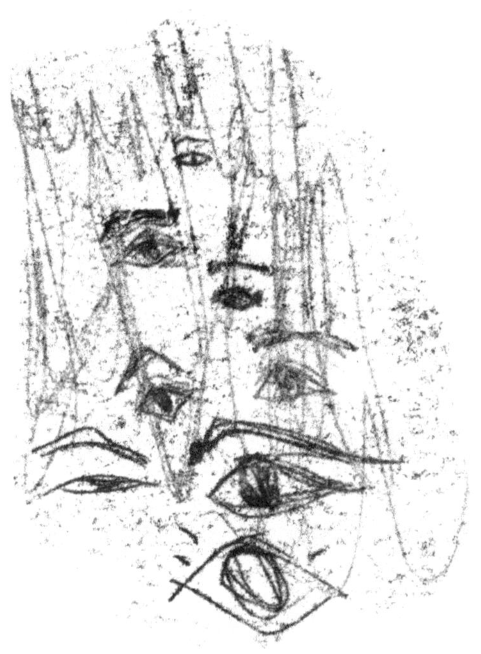

of all the kites
that might take flight in
my skyline
you may be my favorite

I want to live in a world where borders do not
define when we take care of each other
I want to live in a world where we know our women,
girls, children are safe
No matter the country, government,
society they reside in
I want to live in a world that isn't passing their babies
over borders
An assembly line of arms
Carrying an infant to safety
For the front lines of the unknown
are less scary than the known
For the reality is
they are safer alone
than in the country they called home
For no one wants to live in a world
where guns grace doorsteps
and children know
what a war sounds like
what a bomb shelter looks like
what color blood runs
as it leaves a body

I want to live in a world where we choose
each other
over money and power
Where we welcome refugees with open arms
and give them shelter where needed
For we all live on one planet together
We all share the same water, soil, earth beneath feet
love beneath chest
and mind between two eyes
We all share the human experience

You said there are

too many options

With dating apps and social media
we are preoccupied with

too many options

That's why we never settle down
that made me sad
To know that you see us as
'options'
and not people

That's the beauty of love...
despite the options
you still choose each other

Remedies

The sky's full of diamonds
as you drive me home
You say you're taking the long way
so we can be alone
You stopped at every yellow light
till we got
home

His voice is like the crackle of a fire but
the smooth pour of a whiskey glass
Confident and oh so charming
His voice is like an engine
to my body
Starting me up
with every word he speaks
His voice is a silk dagger
A willow tree
Soft yet sarcastic
Bold and witty
A baritone
My favorite note
in any key

I think we put pressure on ourselves
to be loved by everybody else

We fear rejection
it grows in us like guilt
as if we did something wrong
to not be loved by someone else

As if our worthiness
is measured by how many see
our worth

As if beauty is held by the highest bidder

Why do we hold our value
in others acceptance of us

Maybe they couldn't love you
Not because they didn't want to
but because this was a season to love yourself
Unconditionally
Unprecedented
To hold boundaries for yourself
to find that flame
eventually in someone else
But you have to spend time with yourself
be okay with the silence
the stillness that comes from being alone
Sit in your breathing
Listen to your heartbeat
The rhythm of it all
And seasons come like waves in the water
Rippling in
and going out with the tide
Maybe it didn't work out
because something was coming
in the next sunrise

We sleep
Toe to toe
Back to back
My eyes cracked
I am lost in this translation
This comforting ultimatum
This shy yet consuming
Words spoken but not much doing
Love

Your hair is a jungle gym of my hands through it
in the soft sunlight
You put on 'For Emma'
My record player dances
While your fingertips dance along my shoulder blades
We lay in bed
Let the record play
till the end

Love is messy
Love is painful
But Love is kind
in whatever capacity
Love is not hate
Love is the closest thing
We have to magic
And maybe love is not what we picture but what
we feel
When we don't realize it
Love is old friends getting coffee
Love is hands touching
And lips not moving
Love is in hugs and laughter
tears and glasses of wine
Love is a girls night
when you haven't found the right guy again
But love comes in shapes and sizes
So dramatic to what we typically think
Because love isn't always perfect
but that's the beauty

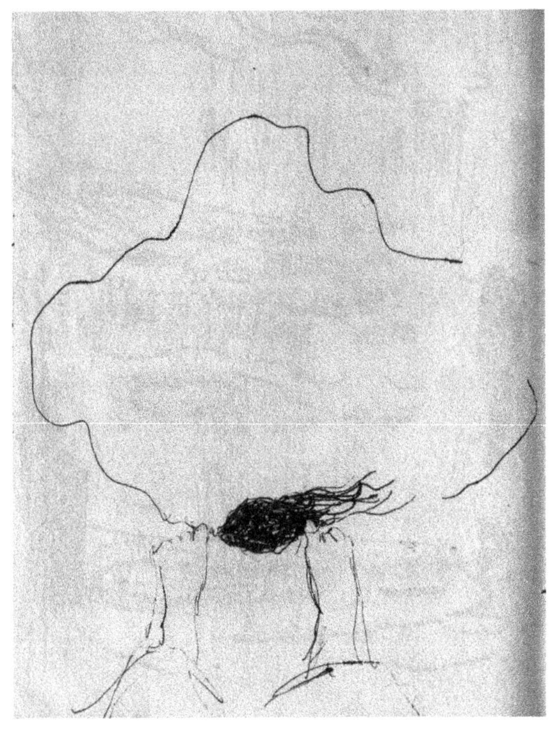

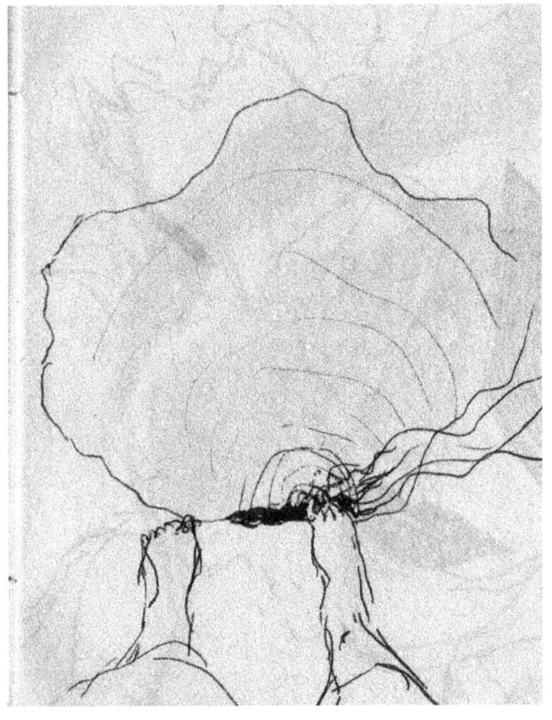

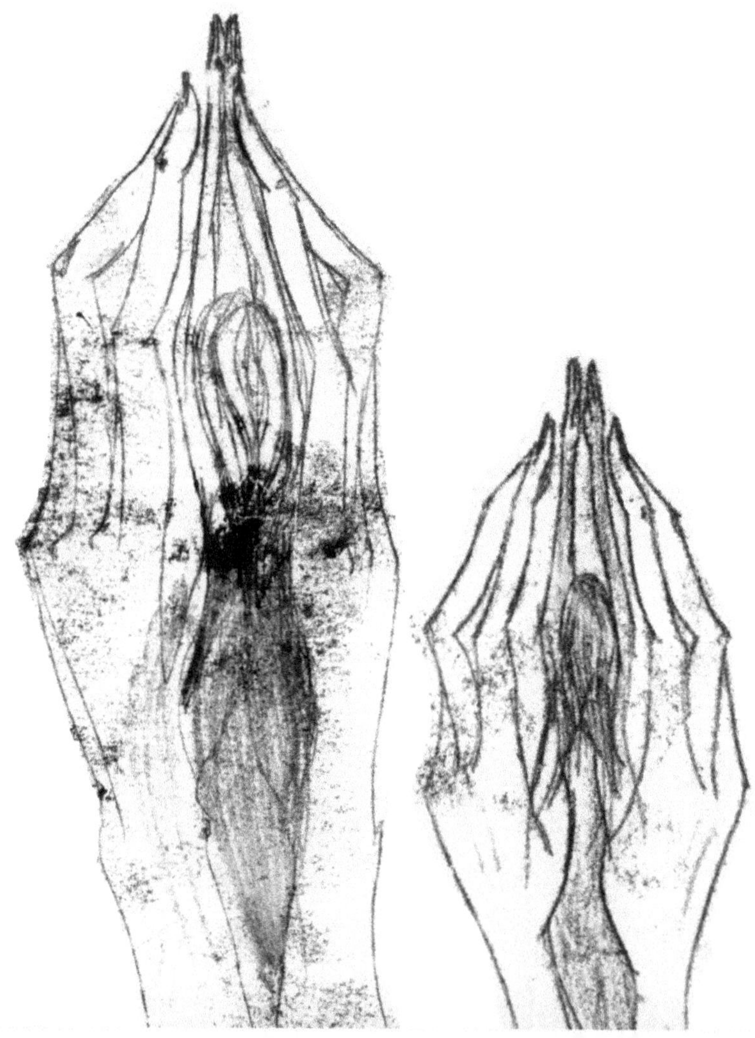

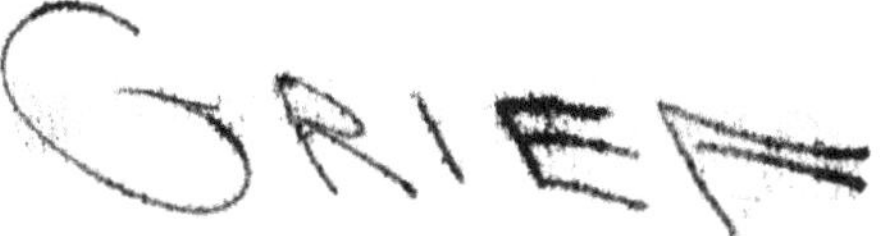

GRIEF

I WILL BE
FOREVER GRATEFUL

remedy for GRIEF

When you've lost someone

Nothing can heal grief, for this I've learned, besides time. But in that time, drink lots of Chamomile tea, write down every memory, move your body, and feel every feeling.

Herbalists suggest that Mimosa flowers and the bark of the tree assist in feelings of loss and grief. It is called the 'tree of happiness' in Traditional Chinese Medicine. It can be found in tea form or infused honey, syrup or tinctures.

Magnesium is said to help aid the body in relaxation and sleep, both things some suffer with when grieving.

I've learned what it feels like to cry so much your eyes become dry and the skin around it starts to peel. I know what it looks like to slowly die - I know what a last breath sounds like.

I know what a hand looks like when it's holding its daughter and its family so tightly as it unwantingly leaves and I know what it feels like to lose your balance at the sight of death. To sit in a corner and wait for the prayer to end.

I know what hospice nurses wear and how they are the kindest people I have ever met. I know what cries of pure sadness sound like and what a parents eyes look like when they've lost a daughter. They never thought they'd outlive their own child.

I know what love looks like - surrounding you as you leave. I know now it comes in all shapes and sizes - in friends and family. I know what illness can do but also what emotions can do to a body.

I know to now let things go, to not hold on so tightly. I know that there is another chapter after this - I know that as a fact, for she told me it.

I know what it's like to see an angel from heaven, gliding through the sky - a shooting star.

I know what it's like to hear someone come back from the other side and whisper who they saw on their way out before they laid back down for their final exhale and we all place our hands around her.

This was it.

The most

PAINFUL

Intangible

Indescribable

HORRIFICALLY

BEAUTIFUL

moment

is when someone knows they will die

And all they can do is say goodbye

Death
Gives life
Value

To know there is an end date
Gives time a purpose
Gives life a purpose
Gives us a purpose
Without death
We wouldn't have life

What happens when the flowers die?
Mother Nature has moved on now
I am left with wilted petals
grieving still what was lost
Between mason jars and elaborate bouquets
scattered across the dinner table
What happens when the flowers die?
Am I supposed to move on or am I supposed to let them sit
there until I can no longer stare at them
Until they no longer can sit within their small vases and must
be pressed into the pages of a book

Like she into ashes
Do I press these flowers to remind myself
of you

My mother

What happens when the flowers die?
Time still moves as fast as it did before
Time does not share discrepancies
Time does not care for the mourning
Time heals on its own
Time kills flowers quickly
But time doesn't heal wounds in haste
Time let's time take its grace

Remedies

I remember driving alone the first time
turning out onto the main road
singing along to my favorite song
it felt too quiet
peaceful
my voice was so much louder alone
an eerie silence
unsettling quiet
without you here it's that same feeling of silence
an echo

    echo

    echo

    echo

    echo in an empty car

Verse- 1   I cried again tonight about you
I didn't want to
So I turned on the T.V.
Tried to watch something funny
To distract myself from the ache
in my gut

The screen flared and the voices
cluttered up my brain
All the crowd laughed
while the sitcom played

Pre- Is it okay that the world lets me distract myself
from you?
I don't have the courage to turn off the room

Chorus- I'll turn on something funny so
I can get out of my head
I'll turn on something funny so
I don't feel this ache in my chest
It isn't working yet

Verse 2-   I cried again tonight about you
I didn't want to
So I turned the T.V. on
Held back the tears till the ads came back on

The jokes numbed my brain
let the shadows play down the hall
While I confined myself to
four white walls

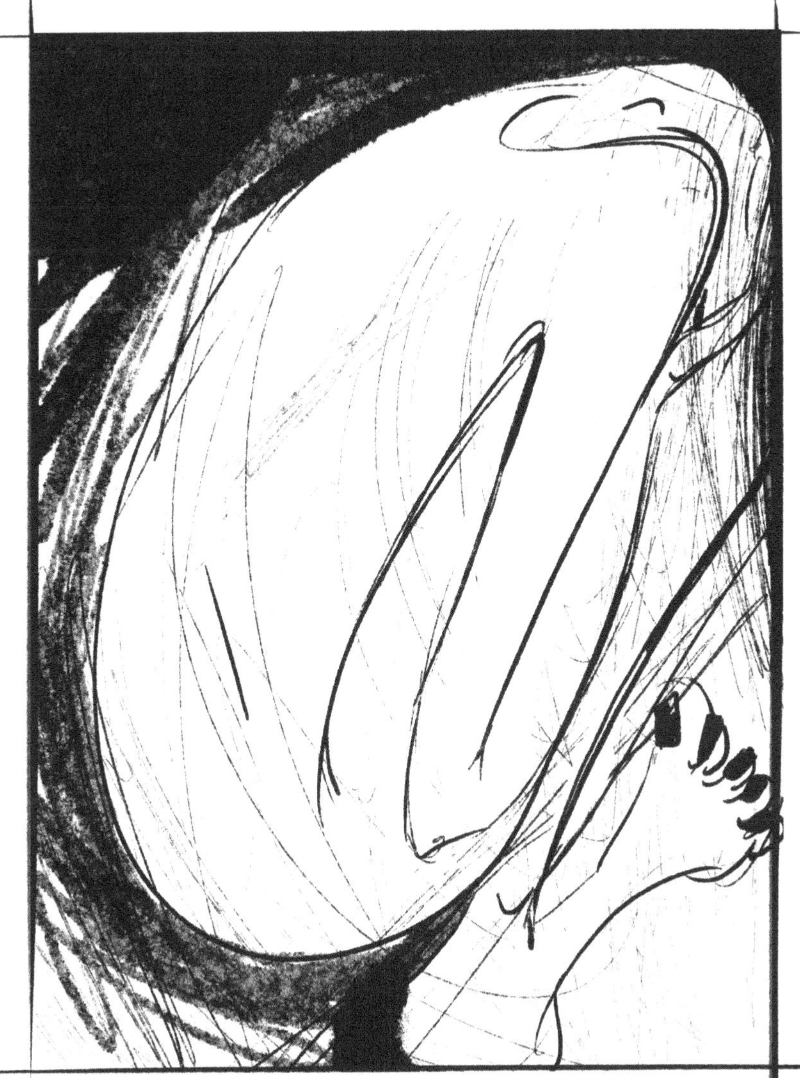

How do you box a scent
How do you keep it on clothes in
drawers
shoes and bags
How do I keep your scent from
airing out of this room
I wish I could make it a perfume
I notice it fade
Every day
I keep the room air tight
Close the door in spite
of the world
How do you box a scent

5 tablespoons
in a box
1 plastic bag full of a person
I believe I should contact the morgue
And ask if they cannot use
Plastic bags
For many reasons
5 tablespoons
of you
spread between us three
among the redwood trees
that's all there is of her
that's all a body amounts to
I guess the soul does travel when the body is burned
I've heard it leaves as soon as it dies
So are these ashes just left in time
An object of bones and skin and eyes
Not of a human
But of what's left
of our kind

You asked me 'why time was so short'

You screamed **WHERE IS GOD**

in a voice deep in your chest
as you lay on the hospice bed

what am I to do without you?

You said

and I laughed and said

what am I to do Without You?

What am I to do without you, now
I feel like a kid when you're sick
at a friend's house
And all you want is your mom
But it's late and your moms asleep
And you feel scared
because it's just you
and the monsters under the bed

WHERE IS GOD
WHERE IS GOD WHERE IS GOD

The winds
Shook our house all night
As planes flew over head
Dumping water over our once green sanctuary

12   dead.
12   dead.
12 dead.

Rings in my ears
He shot 12 dead
One of those numbers
could have been me
at that bar
Dancing to country music
like I used to every Wednesday night
Last night was a Wednesday night...
The sun is setting slowly behind the flames
and smoke
that now grace our once safe home
Eerie and unwelcome
as we sit
in our living rooms
our eyes glued to the news
A mother mourning her son
yells and yells
NO MORE GUNS I don't want prayers I don't want empathy
I want NO MORE GUNS
12 dead.
Wake up and my hometown is now on the list
When will we realize enough is enough
Mother Nature took out her rage in heat
Gracing our hillsides
with smoke and ash and orange flames

now fluttering through the sky
like butterflies
The sun has set now
The smoke has hidden the colors
Soon
We will wake up
and more will be dead
Maybe one of us is next
The sun has set now
The smoke has hidden the colors
Soon
We will wake up
and more will be dead
Maybe one of us is next

I am getting to know you
All over again
Through the eyes and voices and hearts
of other people
Through your handwriting in journals
half finished
In closets full of your scent
and stories told through old friends
and long lost letters read
I am getting to know my mother
in a way I never did before
I thought I was close to her then
But oh the things I get now to explore
I am so lucky to still be able
to get to know her
even after she is gone

A million little daisies
Did bloom on their graves
Along the hillsides
Where flames once scorched their bones
and ours
and every families home
Foundations were crumpled
wood to a match
But a million little daisies
Now stand in place
Of ash

A million little daisies
Did bloom on their graves
Gun to a dance floor
Never be the same
But a million little daisies
Did bloom on their graves
And I stand here
Wondering what the winds had in store for all of you
I wonder if you still had your bones
What would you do
I think you'd do something fantastic
with this life
If you had to choose

Time doesn't move in the house where I grew up
in perfume bottles still standing tall among the
smells of caffeine
like a curtain in her bedroom
Her clothes hang still in closets
Stains on the sleeves of a few
Her socks still sit in the drawers
among all items
Nothing is new
Her voice still echo's from the walls
Her soul running down the staircases
Her hands to work on the kitchen countertops
Time stands still here
So do I
But when I leave
it's like time has said goodbye

The neighbors T.V. blares in the background
My dishwater is way too loud
It drowns out the voicemail I listen to
of you
You sent it October 8th 2020
You said "I am so proud of you"
Its weird to hear your voice

I turn off all the lights and go into my bedroom
Grief doesn't come in stages
It comes in waves, throughout time

I went to a woman yesterday
She said you were in the room
But as you sink into the earth
Day by day
Your ashes become soil
I don't know if I am changing for the better
Or the worse
I endure

And now the neighbors T.V. is getting louder
And the dishwater is on its second spin cycle
I went to a voicemail you sent when you were mad at me
or I at you
I don't remember
All you said was that you're sorry and to remember that
I am loved

Does that love still go behind the grave
There's a space not taken anymore
And I am not knowing what to do to fill it
It's empty

It makes my insides and outsides feel hollow
The world is a few shades darker
now that you're not in it

But does the storm break once the rain stops
or does it come again when the clouds roll in
or maybe that's the lesson
There will always be thunder
but there will also always be sun

You've been sent back
to the veins
rooted between soil
spread out across a canvas
of blue and green and brown
a ball drifting between stars
are you in the stars?
or are you here
or maybe both
stars shine brighter the closer they are
will you still shine for me and vice versus?
now that your gone
can you see my light from heaven?
and can I
see yours?

Veins between family
and veins between earth
a redwood sky
and a sunset birth

Verse 1
Don't wear your favorite clothes
in the hospice room
I wanted to
for you

The red dress with the white flowers
I couldn't find it for hours
But no time on your last morning
to wear your favorite dress in the hospice room

Chorus
But now I feel you in my fingertips
Hear you in my speech
See you in the way I am
and who I am to be
I see you in the treetops
Feel you in the breeze
Dance with you in the words I write
Does heaven grant a guest list?
I will wear your favorite dress
and catch you up on all you've missed
Does heaven have a guest list?

Joy loved visiting the Redwoods at the Santa Barbara Botanical Garden. To honor her memory a commemorative bench has been created in her favorite spot.

You looked at the lady walking across the street
With style and grace - she was dressed head to toe
in Anthropologie
You burst into tears
I want to be that girl again
Will I be that girl again?
With chemo and needles
And pajamas on
I said
Of course you will
You still are that girl
Style is what's on the inside

Dear mom,

2 years of
Holding space for a mother
Who isn't here

2 years of living life
For you
Letting you shine through me
In whatever way you choose
I hold you near me

2 years of letting tears run down my face
I've learned to let it happen
Not to stop the rain
But sit in its peace
There's love in grief

2 years
It doesn't roll off the tongue yet
When they ask when it happened
it feels like it was a lifetime ago
And just yesterday
All in a single sitting
Maybe that's the burden and beauty of time

2 years of making new memories
Without you
It hurts to say that
2 birthdays
2 Christmases
Where I tried
For the family

To be you
Buy the gifts
Fill the stockings
Bake the cakes
Make the dinners

2 years of quiet beach walks
And TV dinners
Ordering in

Of people trying to make me feel as loved
As you did

2 years without your laughter
But I'm learning to laugh alone
The silence doesn't scare me anymore
It makes me wonder
If your home

People talk about the steps grief
like a therapy session
like a planned out plan of action
But no
Grief isn't scheduled
You don't feel shock
Denial
then anger
then acceptance
No you feel it all at once
You feel it not in chronological order
But instead
When your out to dinner with your friends
or on that first date
or alone on a Tuesday night
You feel it in your gut
You feel a sense of fear incomprehensible
of the fact that they aren't here
You see it in your dad's eyes
When he's trying to make you breakfast
like she used to
You feel it in the morning sunlight
when you don't want to get out of bed
6 months after she's past
You feel it all and sometimes none
Sometimes it's like it never happened
and you forget for a minute or two
You think you're unstable
You put pressures on other relationships
To make you feel grateful

No
Grief comes unexpected like a riptide
And all you can do is to try to keep your head
above the water
As it pulls you under

It makes you jaded to your core thinking
life's too short to even care about anything
and at times it makes you feel so alive that you think
everything matters
It's a heightened perception of the world around you
on a constant basis
a honeymoon phase
and then you're left with the pieces of a high

That's what it's like to watch somebody die

The aftermath that follows is one that stays with you
No matter how far you stray
You know what a last breath sounds like
The prayer that follows the silence
The silence that surrounds the room as people
hold on to what was left
Left of us
of you
A death for all
A rebirth

It feels like a new life without you
Maybe it is

But what does soil do the ashes

Does the bark of a redwood

Hold you in it's frayed skin

Your skin to ash

And ash to soil

Do we plant you where the trees are

Or do we spread you across their branches

For we are all more than what we shed

Let bodies rise into nature

and become one

But does the ash bring new leaves

or the same

Are you the tree

or are you the soil

Your eyes, your lips, your smile

So simple and sly

Your scars and hips and fingertips

Ash to soil

And soil to the sea

So you are now a part of everything I breathe

She is so strong
They say
You are handling yourself so gracefully
They say
Through smiles of concern or compassion
The two are unrecognizable
But I am only strong
Because I let myself be weak
in the times I needed to be
I am only brave
Because I let myself grieve
Let myself feel feelings so ugly
Only I could bare to breath them in
And then out
In and out
For grief is not a measuring system
Years marked on calendars
Anniversary of death
March 19th
No grief comes on a Tuesday in summer
Grief stays till your days are outnumbered
Grief sits in your living room
A guest for life
For grief is love
And strength is power
And strength comes from being okay
With being
Weak
Vulnerable
In the eyes of others

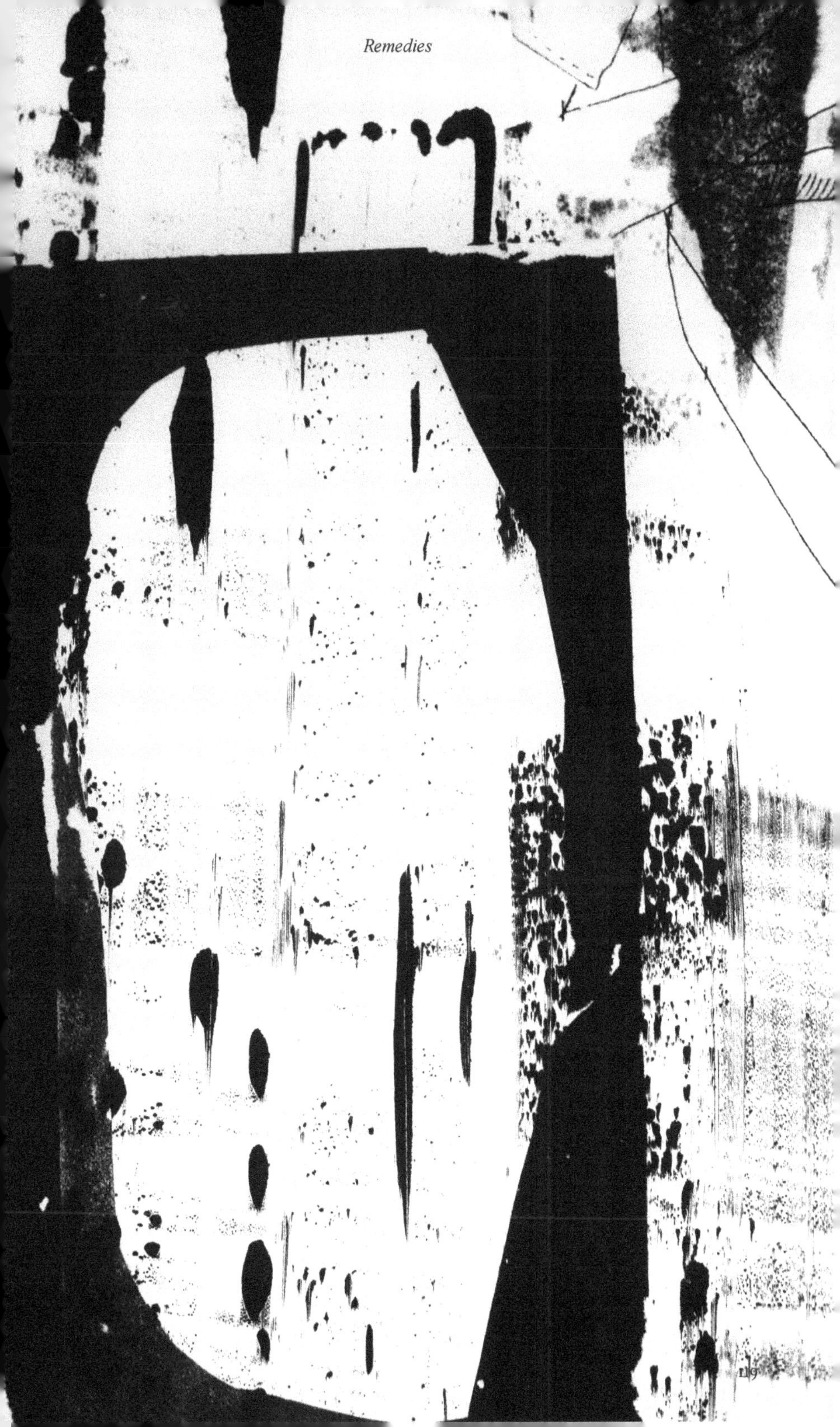

ANXIETY

remedy for ANXIETY

Tulsi tea

The Tulsi plant has been used in Ayurveda, a form of traditional Indian Medicine for thousands of years. It is an adaptogen, a natural herb, which means it helps the body adapt to outside stressors, like anxiety.

Steep one tablespoon of Tulsi leaves,
or a tulsi tea bag, in boiling water.

Cover and steep for 2 to 3 minutes.

Drink and enjoy.

I have a fear of the waves and the water
How the currents can pull me under not able
to come up for air
(I might not come up again)
But I love to pretend I'm in it
I love the smell
and watching the tide roll in
I love to stand in the shallows
Squat
and get my hair wet
I could spend hours
on the shore
and in the white water
But I'm too afraid to go all the way in
Same with love and people
I love to day dream
Pretend the conversations we will have
Pick up on even the little Qs
Highlight them
Bold and red
But I'm afraid
I'll drown
if I dive too deep in
if I get more than my feet wet
Vulnerable and naked
Fully swimming
with no life vest

I was breach

My mother was torn from me

When I was a baby

and now when I am 23

The universe decided me

To lose a mother

Why me

Universe why do you get to decide who stays and who goes

I am lost without a body as a home

Now a soul

A spirit

is all I have to call my own

Mother

I was breach

I was was breach

I was breach

Dear Anika,

How can I begin to describe what it has been like to be "Anika's Mommy" the last 8 weeks? Tomorrow is your 2 month Birthday.

I will start at the beginning. We knew you were breech from week 28. We hoped all along that you would turn. Rasma, the mid-wife, & Dr. Cole, the M.D. encouraged me to have an external version. After much agonizing, I said no. Everytime I thought about it, I would shake, you would shake in my stomach. Your Dad & I felt you were breech for a reason. We were warned that you may have to be born via c-section. I was very afraid to have a c-section but

Today wasn't a good day
But what's a good day measured by
Unless you also measure the bad
For the bad makes the good days feel like a sunset so beautiful
Your feet fall into place perfectly
in everything you do
But today
they didn't
Today they sank into quicksand
while tears cried into a friends shoulder
over things maybe not worth my energy
Today my body sank into the idea that it would be just that
a bad day
Because sometimes being sad is comfortable
Sometimes being depressed
is comfortable
It can be uncomfortable to say to yourself
I'm going to get out of this funk
Get out of this bed
and move on with the day ahead
with what's left of daylight

I can feel you in the floorboards
creaking as I walk
I can feel you in the windows
looking in at every nook
And I can hear you in my bedroom
waking me up at night
Oh how you like to play
with my mind
and leave me like
a ripped out book

Fear
You're an old friend
You used to hide
under my bed
Fear
You've found me again
but those times need to come to an end
Fear
You're an old friend
but I have to say goodbye

I still hear you
in the back of my brain
Wreaking havoc
on everything I say
and I still feel you in the passenger seat
Directing me where to go
not letting me leave
this town

I can see you in my car
smiling as we don't go very far...

I'm not scared of dying
I'm scared of forgetting people

and what they said
how they made me feel
I'm not scared of dying
I'm scared of not living

I'm not scared of love
I'm scared of reliance
I'm good on my own
I don't need to try it

I'm not scared of dying
In fact, I'd like to try it
Just to know what to expect at
the end of everything
Is that an option?

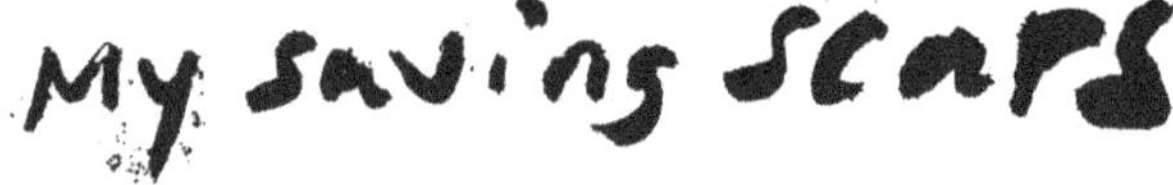

My eyes in hindsight

Marked up and down my arms
You ask what they are
I tell you

My bruised ego
My confidence combustion
My heart that always falls
For the wrong kinds of 'something'
My maybes grace the dinner table
More than my promises
I'm stuck with fork and knife
to all the words I never said

I used to think the war was outside my bedroom window
Ran scared to bed right after 9
But my mother came and said
Don't worry dear
The war is far away from
here
But she was wrong
There's also a war right outside
My windowpane shakes with the times
and every body that hits the halls of a school floor
may disagree with her too
There's a war in our backyard

I used to think the war was outside my bedroom window
Ran scared to bed hid under the sky
My little suburb
was under attack
By AK-47s shot by an 18 year old boy
Blood is now spilled in my backyard

But we are too transfixed
on screens
To look up and see
the news is on us now

I never feel this feeling
These stones in my gut
but when you gave me words of affirmation
and made it clear you wanted us
I now have a gravel driveway leading up to all my thoughts that
are overflowing
of possible rejection and all the things
I think I'm not

I am leaving only when
My blisters have healed
and the construction on my favorite street
has ended
And when the baby chicks I saw first born
are now standing
Only a week later

Part of me wishes
to stay longer
Only now that things have healed
and I've gotten my footing
and I feel
alive
But maybe there was beauty
in the healing
And that makes all the difference
Maybe I came here to heal the
blisters
and grow new
skin
Only to go back to the world I live in
I checked in on New York
and New York has checked in on me
and we are both doing
just fine

79
Street

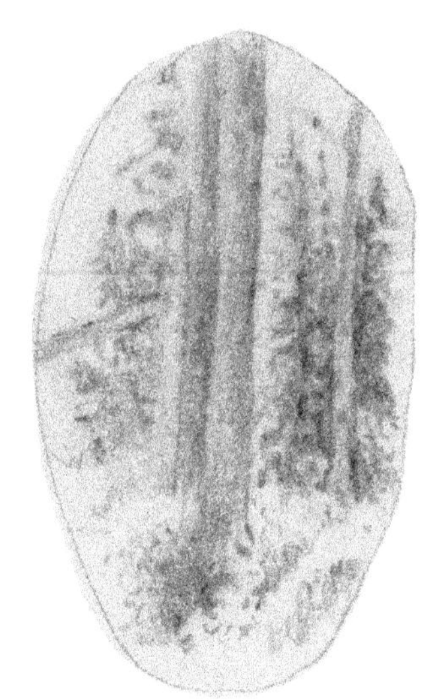

Snow like fingers
Running across the sierras
Dancing with the redwoods
and whispering with the winds
Snow like fingers
Cascading across white landscapes
Inching their way to the base
of each canopy of rock
Each bark of stump
Until the whole world
is covered in white
Cold and brisk and quiet
Air as sharp as a butter knife

I wish to be a mountain

Even when flames scorch its hillsides

It's foundation stands

and grows back

even more beautiful than before

burned out
Ich liebe
dich!

Remedy for when the  hurts

Echinacea is an all around tonic for wellness and rejuvenation. When we feel our bodies are down, we nourish with herbs that support our immune system and bring back balance to our lives. Echinacea supports the body physically but also emotionally, keeping a clear mind and an open heart.

Another remedy to sooth the heart is rosemary. Try a rosemary tea and take the time to grieve and find a new source of joy.

Love. It's a weird thing. More than a verb, sometimes less than a noun, always an adjective to describe how fast our hearts race. It can linger longer than some may like, like that old stain on a favorite shirt or it can go through some faster than alcohol - all you have left is the hangover to prove it. You were a verb, noun, adjective, all at the same time. Kept me running to the next finish line, only to realize your love was not the prize. Your love was unattainable, although I thought I was the mystery piece for you to all of a sudden need.

But my love for you was a pronoun. Always available to you, a Hallmark greeting card.

Under a scaffold sky
and concrete parks
Under glass ceilings
and metal lined stars
I keep you here
lined with orange tape
"Under construction"
reads across your face
I'll return
When I'm
ready

waiting for you

Fireflies danced around us
The whole night
As if watching
and waiting
Hoping their light
Would spark something
I still craved
Between the two of us

All of your wounds
Ripe for the picking
You say
You won't go down that road again
No scabs will be picked
No veins reopened
All memories sealed
in plastic bags
With plastic people

Wounds ripe for picking
are wounds fresh
but wounds fresh
Should be tended too
I say
But you cover it up with a band aid
and say it shall bleed out on its own
No one to help
No one left to hold
or puncture another wound

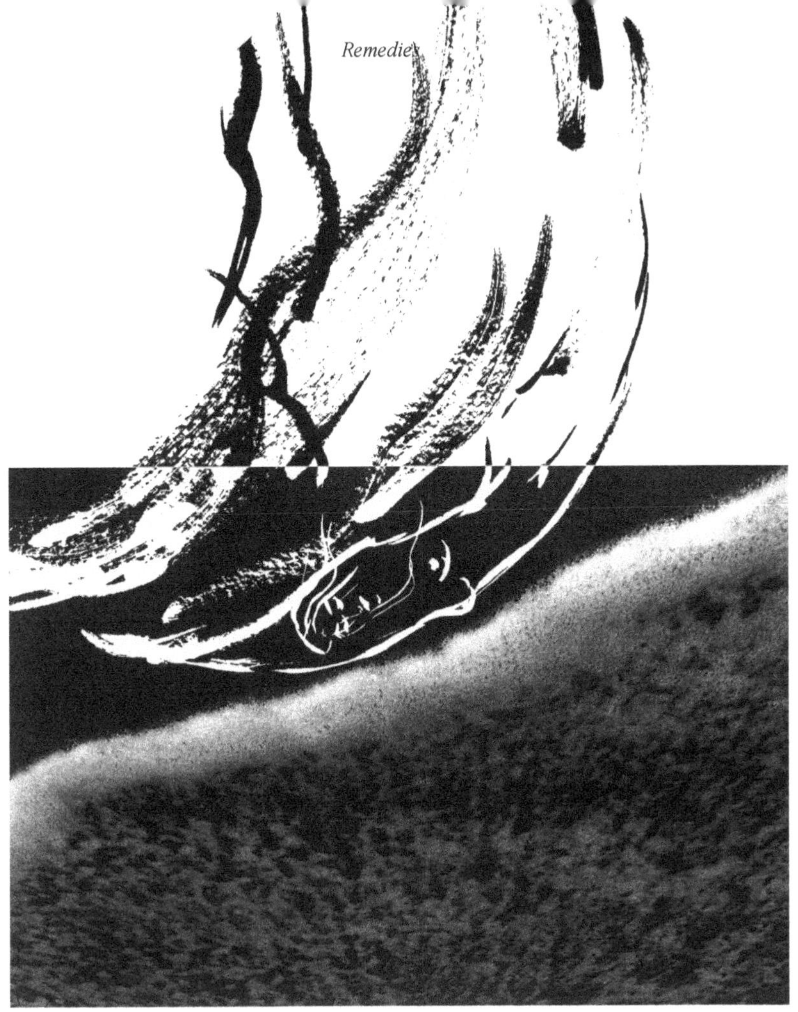

I'd rather be friends
with the currents
than you
You change your mind more than the oceans do

I think you could have loved her beautifully if
You'd tried
Did you know how much she loved you
For I think if you did maybe you wouldn't
be so scared to love her back
We all have our pasts that have broken us
in places we don't want to now fix
But one day
I hope you may let someone in
But for now
You only make 'friends'
A friend can't hurt you the way a lover can
No
A friend won't hurt you the way a lover can

But that's a lonely way to live

He's moved home
My voice quivers
My knees buckle
The thought of your tongue around
my neck
seems to lick away
all the storms
you've brought to my bay
My boats
and harbors
and houses
weren't built
for such winds

He's moved home
dropped out of college
My eyes throttle
as I walk
Thinking I see you
at every turn and bend
The waves are a little bigger
Tonight
Thunder shook my window pain
And lighting struck the once wispy
Angelic clouds

Why has he moved home?
My heart asks my head
It's not for you my darling
Remember
You've moved on instead
But the rain is still knocking
On my roof in the morning

And the trees have cried their leaves off
Made a mess of my front yard
And there's puddles in the alley ways
The boats are rocking
Side to side to side

How bored they must be
Those people who found love
Instantly

I want the house with the biggest tree on the block
It doesn't have to be fancy
Perhaps a willow tree
And flowers upon flowers
And a porch with a swing
A place for the cat to sleep
I want the house that changes color
In the spring to summer to fall
Red leaves coat the lawn
I want the house where the parties are thrown
And people are always home
Where the kitchen smells of pancakes and coffee
And the door is always open
And the sun comes through the windows
All day long
I want the house where the family lives
and the kids play outside till the tables set
I want a house on a walking street
With a little box out front
Full of books I don't need
It doesn't have to be the nicest
Nor the biggest or the most pristine
I just want the house where the birds come to sing

You wanted me
When your life felt lonely
When she had left and you thought you needed
Someone
You wanted me when your life was quiet

But I wanted you in the turbulence
When the earth shakes your footing
And nothing feels right
But
I wanted you when the chaos still ensued
I wanted you through it all
That was the difference
Between us
I wanted you to soothe the noise
While you wanted me to disrupt the quiet

Girlfriend
No one has ever given me that title
They have given me
"good friend" "my girl" "this is her"
They have put me in a corner of
"sitationships" "flirationships" "we're just hanging out"
"Their secret when their friends are around"
They have given me excuses of
But I'm not ready to let you go yet
I'm not in a stage to be tied down
But I want to see you
Take you on dates
Nice dinner in Silverlake
Table for two
For maybe down the line you could be my Girlfriend
But just not now
They tease with the word
But never I who gets to wear it
Why is it that I am to always be
"More than a friend but not more"
My friends are someone's girlfriend
And boyfriend
Partner
Spouse
I would like a name
I'm proud to say aloud
to know I am somebody's

The sand beneath toes
Like grains of stories you told
Slowly piling up to who you are
Who you may be
If I let you in
Like the tide every morning
Salty serendipitous moments
Clogged pores like clogged airways
at your presence
I lose what I wish I could say
Rough ridges like rocks in the water
A rugged map to where you leave or
stay
My fingers leave
Imprints in the sand
While our toes play footsie
Under earths own hands

You said writing lets you taste life twice
Maybe that's why I haven't been able to write
I haven't wanted to relive him twice
Through my pen
onto paper
I'll save writing about him
For later

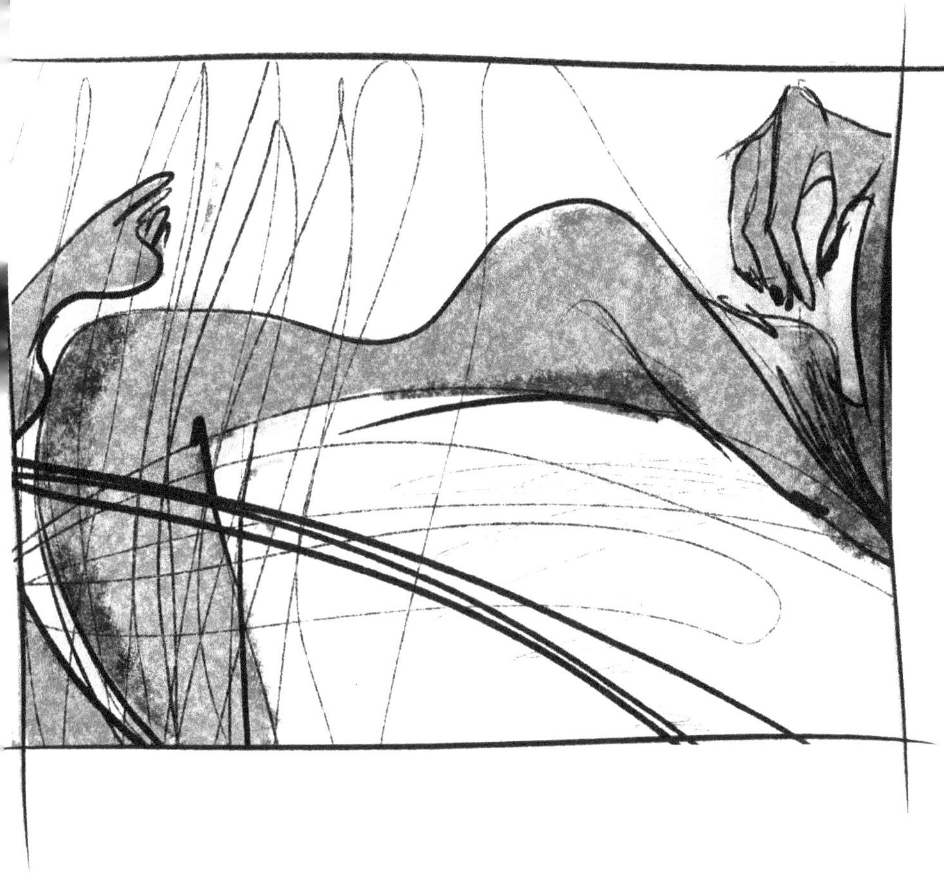

I made ripples
in your waters
I brought currents
reefs
and life
You in turn
brought waves
and riptides
Tsunamis
and Mavericks
But you blame me
for the floods and the storms

Do you think I was the country
With my arms stretched wide
Did you think I was a river
Comfortable enough to hide in
Did you think I was a vacation
fly back on the next red eye
Did you think I was a Holiday Inn
Only good for one night
No, I'm home
I want to be home
I'm a one-way ticket
Once you're on the plane
You should be
All in
I'm an ocean
Far deeper than you care to go
So don't think I'm a shallow pool
of little water
Mostly stones

He didn't know his own purpose
So how was he to understand
The purpose of you

He huffed and puffed with an air of confidence.
He knocked only once and left a bouquet of flowers.
They were prickly and left petals all over my carpet.
They smelled of him and day old flowers.
He was smooth, like a butter knife but
a mosquito bite - itchy.
He was a wool sweater I couldn't wait to take off.
Dead flowers in a clear vase.
No water left in its place so I had to throw them away.

ITS
ALRIGHT

I am a piece of art
You were just too busy
Staring at the whole gallery
To ever look in depth at
The strokes across my canvas
or the colors
You didn't see me
You saw what I am from a first glance
as your eyes danced from one canvas to the next

I am a piece of art
You were just too busy
Bidding on the whole gallery
To ever look in depth
at the cracks in my canvas
or the colors underneath
You didn't see me
You saw what I am from first glance
as your eyes danced from one canvas to the next

What will I be

He lent me his poetry book
The one he thought I'd like

It's now sitting on my sofa,
Bukowski
Love is a dog from hell

The smell of him throughout the pages
With corners he marked down
Said, I wonder if you'll know why
I marked certain ones
I laughed and joked it was a game

He lent me his poetry book
First edition
He liked to keep first editions

Bukowski
Would have liked us
The dull moments
Filled with drama in each crease and crevice
He would have found pleasure
in the vainness and pain of it all

No strings attached
or maybe there were
They were just invisible
A spider's silk
of so many words
I forgot what was spoken
and what was not

A web of thoughts and feelings caught

You cannot discard me
Like a cologne bottle
Once you've used up all the scent
I am more
Than what you think of me
I am breath
Bones
Heartbeat
Heat between thighs
Beat between breasts
I am human

Don't ever let someone's inability to love you
Become the doubt in loving yourself

BULLYING

Remedy for when people aren't kind

Rose water is beneficial for self love.
It brings awareness back to the body and
a refresh to the soul.

Homemade rose water
1 ½ cup water
fresh roses

Directions
Remove petals until you have 1 cup of roses.
Combine 1 ½ cup water and your roses in a pot
and bring the water to simmer.

Once simmering, reduce heat and leave for 20 minutes or
until the petals have lost their color.

Strain or use a muslin cloth to separate the petals
and the rose water.

Character is defined by how you react
to what you've been given.
how you act in reactions,
how you treat others when life isn't going
your way...
despite everything
you've been thrown.

Character is how you treat others
despite how they treat you.

Does your injustice provoke justice?
Does your violence toward violence
end violence?
Two wrongs do not make a right.

She used to be
Someone I admired
Looked up to
Like a glass jar
To a light
Saw fireflies inside
And decided I'd open the lid
And let them take flight
Didn't realize
Your light
Was dictated by others
Once appraisal was gone
You were out for another
Your worth was judged
By how many you could carry
You loved the attention
And mustered up the best fairies
to light you
Only befriend those who benefit you.

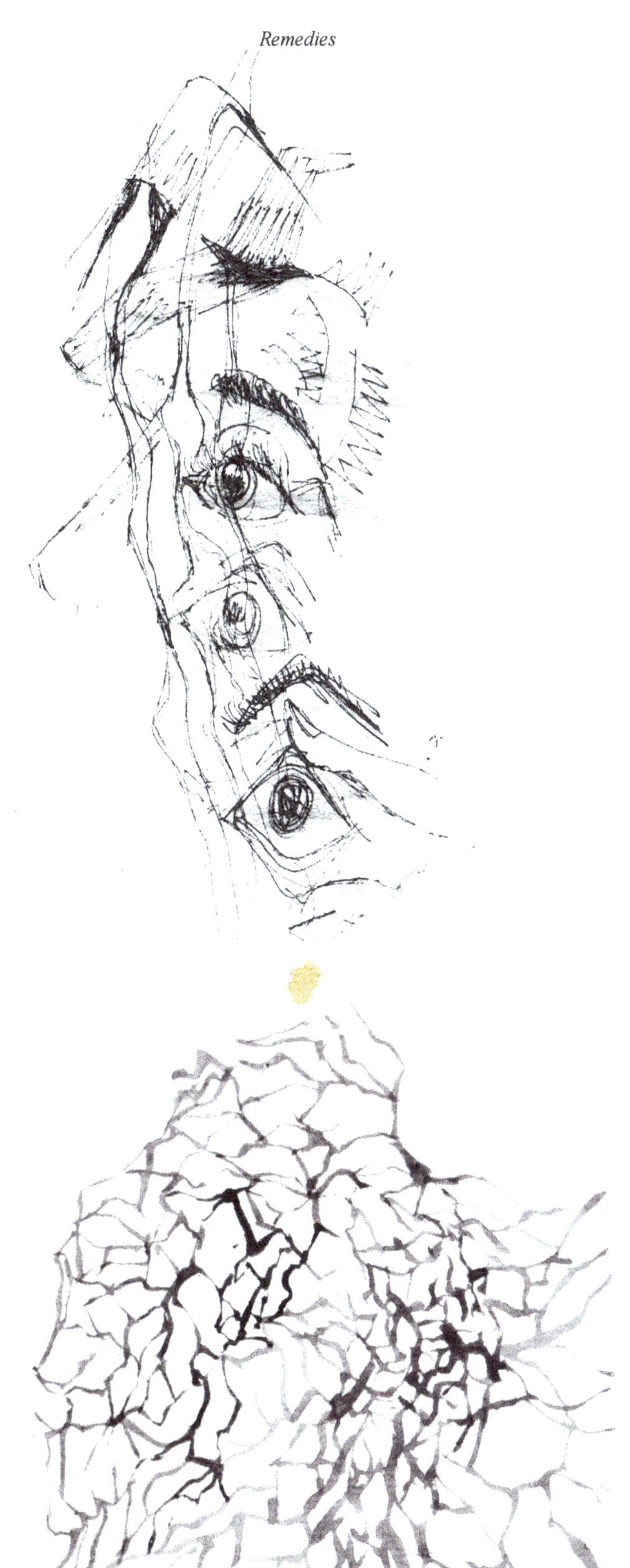

They came with rubber bullets
Watered down news
Flares and tear gas
"Light 'em up" they screamed
as they marched through
They came with bullet vests
And military arms
For people with cardboard signs
We came with
words as weapons
The voices of lives taken
Carried through our own
A walk across a nation
We came with hearts full
and hands shaking
each other's
of togetherness
And blistered feet
walking miles to show how we should treat
a human race
We came with paper and a sharpie
and you came with pepper spray

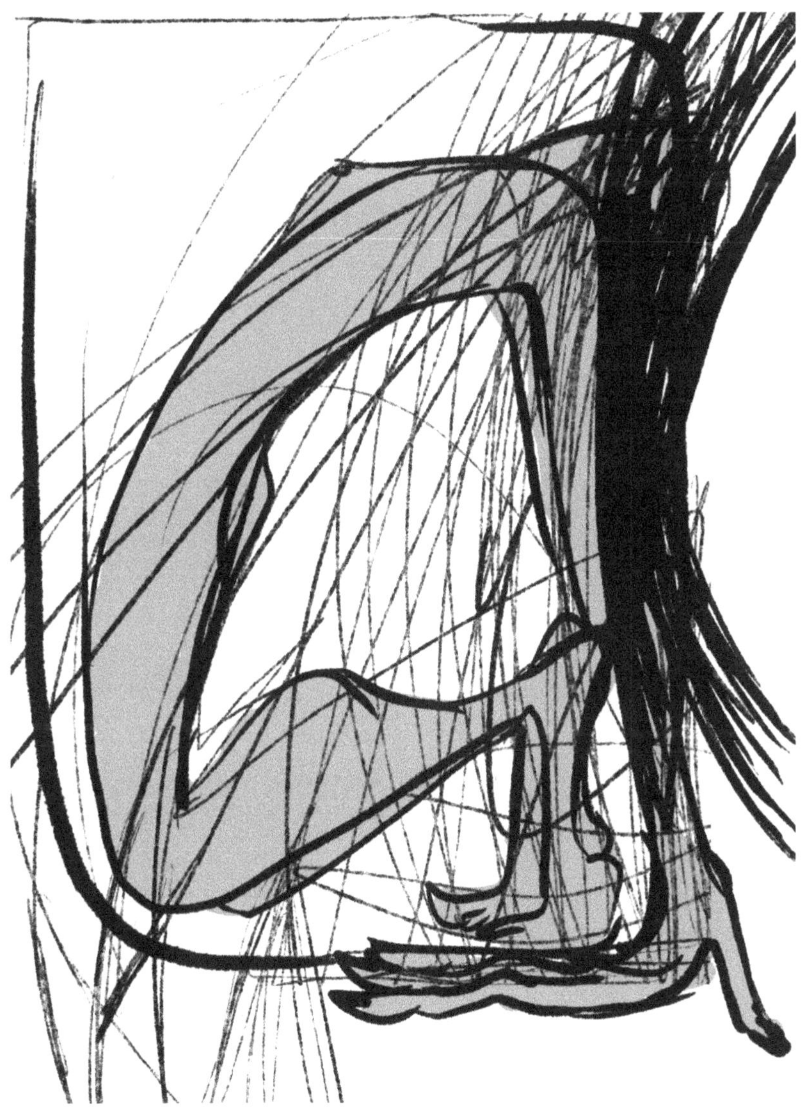

There is a line between
Selfless and self-righteous
Of concern over calculation
Of compassion over comfort
Power vs. possession
There is a line between
Fear over empathy
and rules over what's right
of action over the reaction
and lack thereof over love

She defames
My character
Out of ignorance
Of her own
She is a shell of a person
Trying to find homes in
others
Self pity
No insurance
Of who she will become
Selfish to implore
Her own world
of who succumb
I feel sorry
For women
Who tear others down
to build their own throne

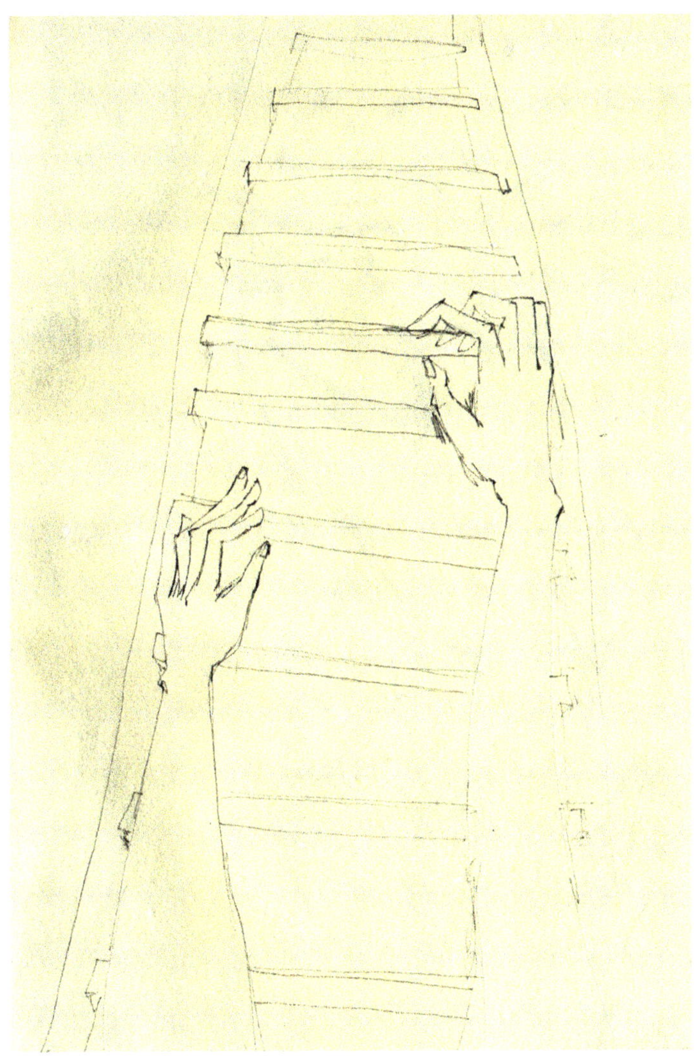

I am my mother's bones and breath
I am my mother's
Warmth in the rain
And a kiss on a forehead
I am my mothers
voice in a crowd
I look for her in supermarkets
Aloud I say
I am my mother
But where is she
She is sewn into the fabrics of me
Every outline and memory
A reflection of who she was to be
is to be
Within the seams of my actions
Of my words
I am my mother's blood
And skin and hair
And eyes
We didn't look alike
But from the inside
We were one
Are one
I am my mother
I am so proud to be
To call her love
my best remedy
And on days when I feel she is so far away
I can look upward
To the trees
"You will see me"
whispers the leaves

But if he was real
If he was out there
Looking down on us
Wouldn't he give us a sign?
Wouldn't a God want us all to know He is there?
Wouldn't a Creator want credit for His work?
No
There are hints in the smallest things
In the shapes of leaves
In the way the sun heats but never burns
How the ground rebirths
How everything has a complex
System of measurement
of art
Behind it all
But He is a selfless creator
Who doesn't need validation for what He has done
He doesn't need fame to feel loved
We should all strive to be like that

If a tree falls and no one's there to listen
Does it make a sound?
If I speak into the silence
But no one is around
Does my voice really make a sound?
Am I heard
Even when no one is around

Do I need an audience
To make an impact

In the darkest times
I've seen the most love
My dad to my mom
His consistent heart and steadiness
Grounding us all
My aunt who dropped everything
To fly across the country
help in any way she could
The doctors who gave us a place to
stay, a hope to hold onto
And the friends who are a shoulder
A rock
in the darkest times
I see the most good
As long as you let a little light in

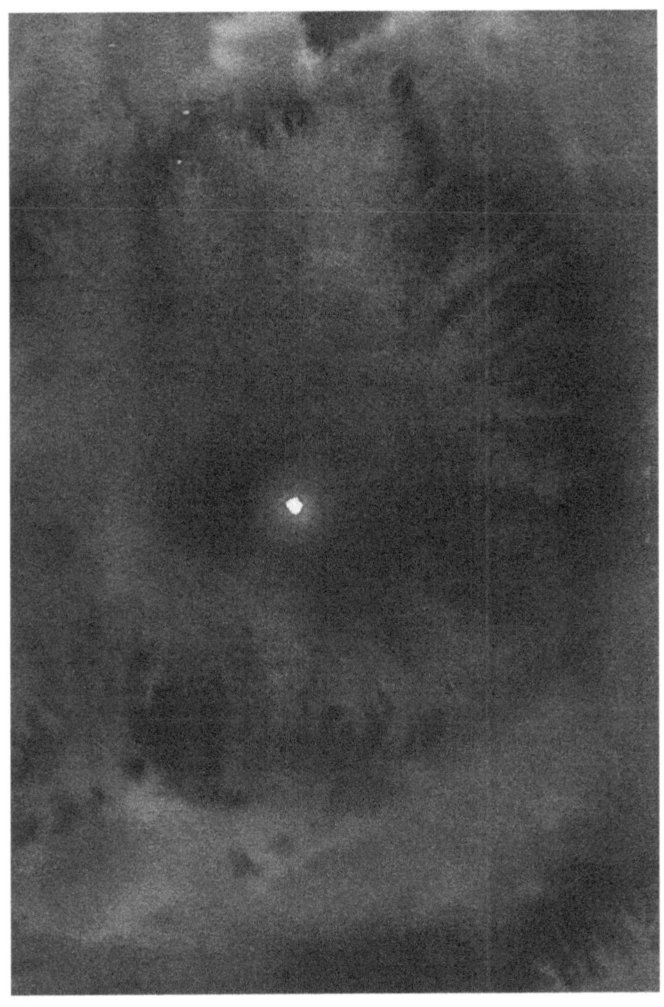

My eyes have been fountains
But they water the seeds
of what I should grow
And what I should leave
My eyes have been fountains
Since your body left me
But your soul is above
Watering me

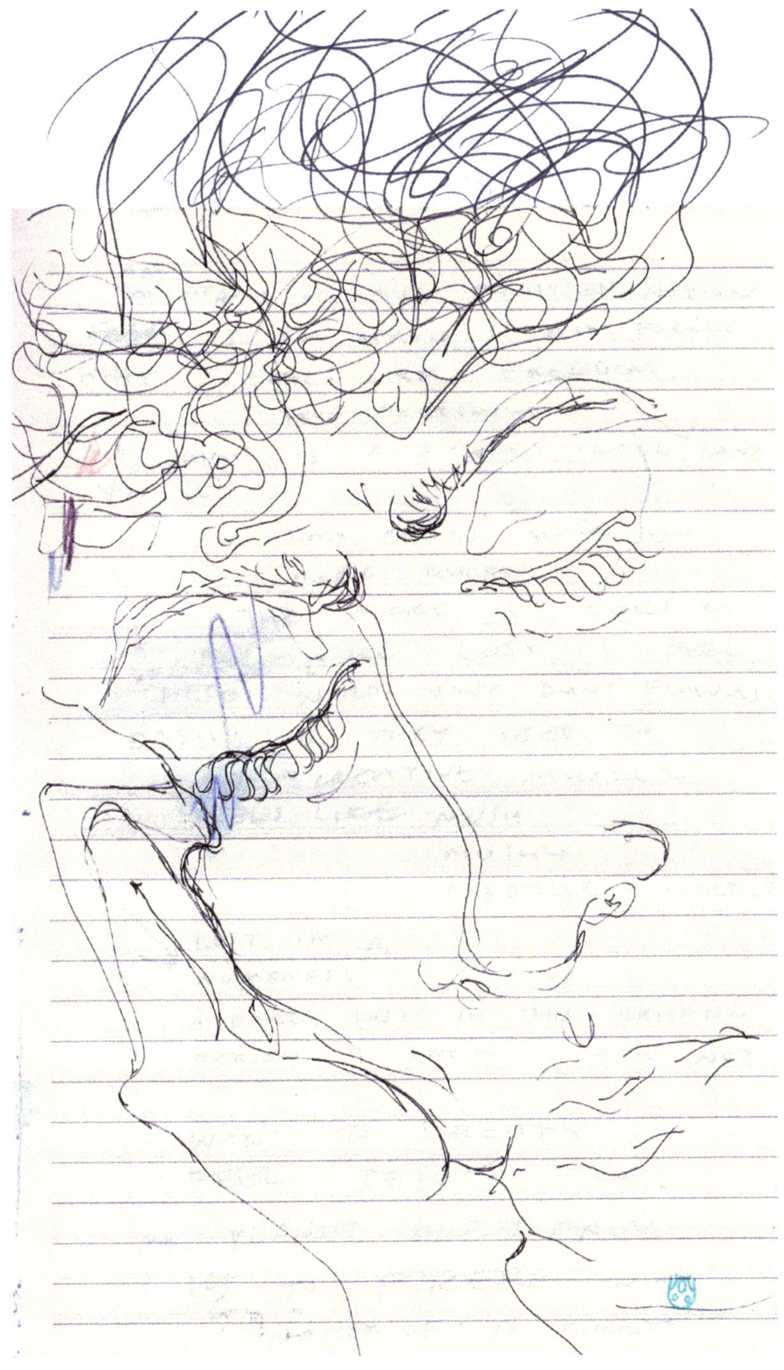

I never asked for your opinion
On my look
Perfume
Outfit of the evening
Late at night
at a bar
I never asked for your opinion
So why do you think it's warranted?
I never asked for your attitude
And when I gave it back
I am instead called 'sassy' 'rude' 'must be on her period'
'why are you getting so defensive?'
When really I only said what you said, as a man
But as a woman, we are called words and phrases that
do not match
The gender equality of the two of us
I did not ask for your flirtatious looks
Cat calling
And demanding behavior
I will not stroke your ego
Be polite
To get attention from a man
at a bar
Late at night

She was a weeping willow
Extending her love across ponds
And rivers
Valleys and forests
Her leaves touched everyone in her path
Even when the winds changed course
Her branches would sway ever so gracefully
As not to harm anyone
In her way

her path

course

so gracefully

But if the trees could talk
Would we listen
If the tress could talk
Would we see
If the tress could talk
Would it make a difference?
Would we have more empathy?

You live beneath a scaffold sky
You do not know
How real stars' shine
You cannot see
The moon lit night
Or the orange brush
Water coloring the morning
You do not know
What is real
You see from your perspective
But there is far more out there
Than what's above your head
Beneath your feet
Beyond what your two hands
Can reach
You live beneath a scaffold sky
Where grey and blue and green
Match the colors in your shallow eyes
You may be born
Under what blocks you
But know there's more
Than what those living under
A roof of construction
Tell you
You are

Your God is not my God
I think He stole my Gods seat in the sky
With racial slurs
And shots fired
From a gun you bought at a Walmart
Your God is not my God
I think He stole my Gods seat in the sky
With hate crimes
And a world of order
Love confined
And so so many borders
If we are all made in the eyes of Him
Why do you think you can judge?
Why do you think
You've got a right to the gavel

Remedies

GROWTH

Remedy for   GROWTH

Walnut is the remedy to help protect us against outside
influences in general, and against the
effects of change in particular.

Walnut Bach Flower Remedy
Directions
2 drops on your tongue
Will help with the ability to adapt to change.
Also many long walks and being outside
always helps the mind.

You say I've changed
Good
I'd hate to be the person I was before
That means I'm not

Growing

Mother Nature

Is burned

Soaked

Tumbled

And washed away

But still grows back

Patiently

And slowly

Taking its time to grow

Each weed, daisy, mountain

At a time

I live in the small moments
Not the big moments
I live in the silence of a car between songs
I live for eye contact between someone you love
Across a dinner table
I live for good wine and good company
Together on a Friday evening
I live in the moments of laughter
At a family reunion
And the feet dancing across the floor
All in unison
Blood runs above water
And the web of family
Will never go under
I live for community
Knowing your neighbors

That sense of belonging
I live for dinner parties in the front yard
And that sound of forks across plates and glass clinking
Cheers to another evening
I live in the small mundane moments
Waking up to someone you love
hidden under linen
A cup of homemade coffee
I live in the slow pace of road trips
Drives up north to be with mom in the treetops
I live in the moments of grieving
I live in the moments of leaning
Where your feet may not be that steady
But there is meaning
Behind it all

I believe life can be hectic
And still
in a single moment

Where one walks by
Underneath clouds of storm
Unaware of what the neighbor is crying of
A wall between them

While one loves and one hates
in a single room
Miscommunication between them two

And one births in a hospital room
While another dies in a hospital room

The trees sway frantically
The window rattles
But the poems are read on a porch swing
A roof above my head
Still
Yet brewing

The yin and yang
The ebb and flow
The balance of it all

Not being happy with the small things
Always needing more
Will lead to not being happy with anything
And constantly looking for

More

You will constantly strive for what's
better in your eyes
Instead of realizing and being grateful for
what's in front of you

My mom wanted a house in the redwoods
Full of pine needles and trees and branches
Climbing through the living room
She wanted windows upon windows
Looking out upon the view
My dad wanted to grow old with my mom
He wanted a partner for life
Someone to love his wrinkles and his graying hair
Someone to be there for every big life moment
From the start to finish
I wanted a mom to be there on my wedding day
I wanted my kids to say the word "grandma"
I wanted someone to lead the way
We don't get everything we want in life
But that just makes what we do get all the more special
It makes all the moments all the more priceless
It makes all that we feel
All the people we love
All the things we are given
Feel like little miracles

I've built up a wall
I stare at myself through a white wood lined mirror
9 am Paris
I've become hard
My actions start to spill out of my mind
Like muddy water from a dirty tap
I have not been myself
It's cold outside
Fall brisk
And the neighbors are looking out through their
flower lined windows
I've made myself so indestructible
My heart cannot pass
To others
I've slaved away at barriers
So even the smallest enemy
Will not touch me
It's 9 am
The mirror is fogged up from my shower
My decisions are spilling out of me
And the water is only slightly muddy now
The tap is still running
I take a deep breath
Chip chip chip away
The hardness from within
The water is a small shade of grey now
My heart, not a weapon
My hands, not a dagger
My voice, not a shield
9:30 am
My makeup is on
I'm dressed in the mirror

I've let the actions of others upon me
Dictate who I think I need to be
Angry pessimistic cynical untrustworthy
Eventually
The water will be clean

You said trees won't grow
Without a little wind
For wind makes them strong
Holds them up
as they get taller
For wind tests the trunks
Builds them up
Keeps them whole
For if the wind didn't shake its branches
It wouldn't know how to continue to stand
After one storm

Sometimes I like the past
I wrap myself up
in its down comforter
Sing myself to sleep
With old pop songs
From the early 2000s
I'll put it on and wear it
Like armor for the future
I'll wrap it up
Gift it
To someone I'd forgotten
I'll reminisce
Put on glasses
That remind me
of summer days at the lake
and nights spent under oceans covers
I'll let it kiss me
When I'm lonely
And hold its hand
When I'm afraid
I sometimes like the past
But it has a way of taking time away
From the future

There's a moment
When you realize that
everything you used to be
became everything you should be

Growing up doesn't always mean getting wiser

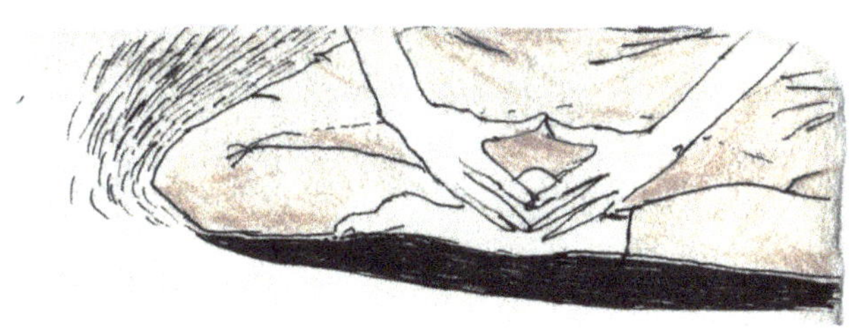

Stop waiting for things to happen
Drink that bottle of wine you saved for a special occasion
Tonight is
Love the people you are scared to
Time is shorter than we think
Drive up the coast spontaneously
What is planned sometimes rarely happens
And that road trip can't wait
Go to the trees
They are good for the soul
No matter how far the drive is
Cry in friends arms
Even if you are embarrassed to

The best friends are the ones that comfort you
And the things you wait for the perfect moment for
Rarely happen
Because nothing is perfect
So the moment is now
Or never

Sometimes
We need someone
To come along
With gardening gloves
And a shovel
Yank these deep roots
Out of the ground
Dig us a new hole
And plant us on higher
Sun washed ground
Help us move on
From the soil we grew around

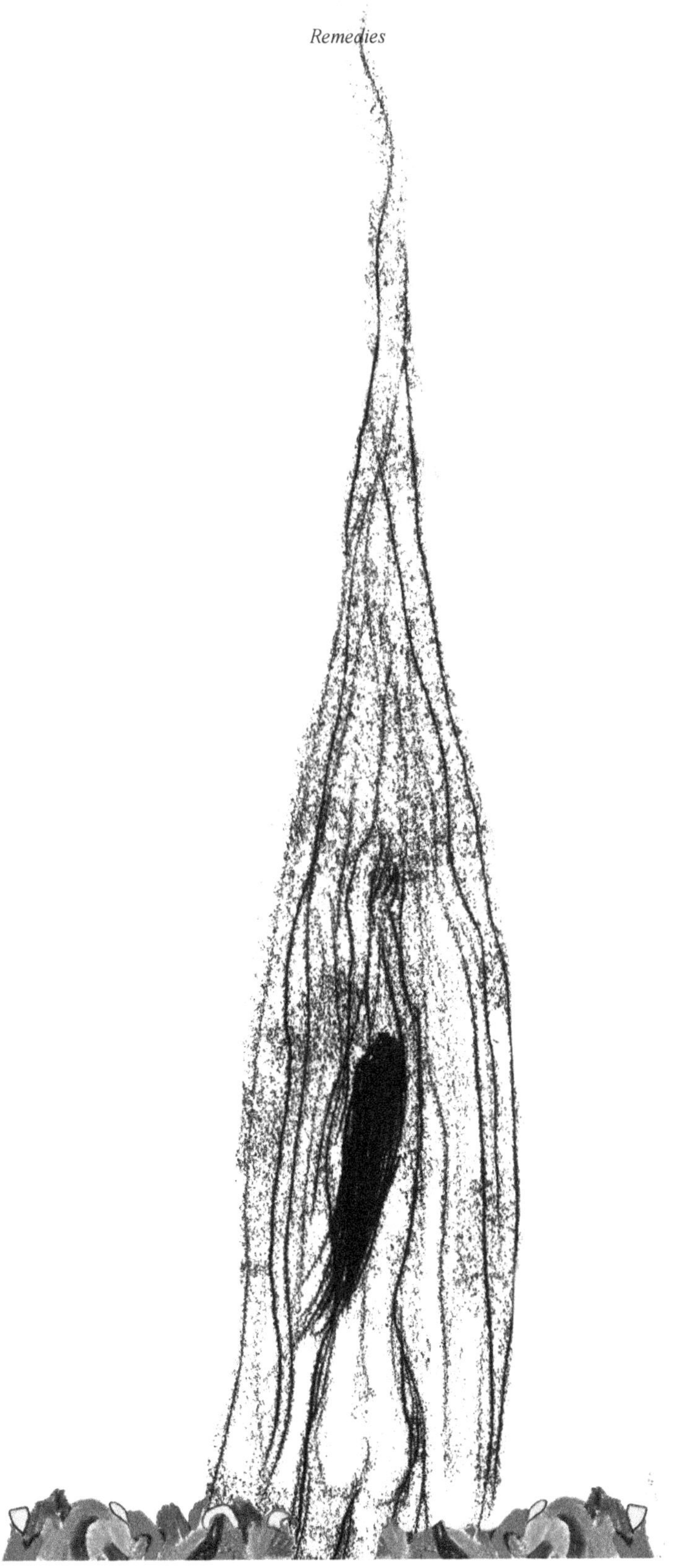

Life is like the seasons
One moment
You're happy
Warm
Vibrant
Sitting with life on a sandy beach
the next your shedding
You feel yourself aging
You feel yourself wilting
with all that you carry
Your leaves are changing
Ready for a new chapter
in life
The prospect of getting older
makes your tree of life
begin to shake and cry
Red orange and brown
fill the front yard
Then, you're cold
depressed
Trying to figure out what to do next
in life
But there are moments
when you lie in the snow
make snow angels
even in the dead of winter
you go ski
and find peace
in the discomfort
Things aren't going the way you like
but just like that
spring comes
and you're noticing a mood change

things are looking up for you
and before you know it
your sitting with life on that sandy beach
rejoice
it's a journey all over again

My mother died the day before spring
Maybe if she lasted another day
The buds would bloom
And she'd take a turn towards the dew
And get better
Or maybe
It was her way of telling me
To rebirth
And let the sun
Still come through
After this long winter

THINGS I HAVE LEARNED THIS YEAR

Life is short
And time isn't fair
But it's all the more bittersweet
People are like the tide

They ebb
        and flow

so don't hold on too tightly
Things fall apart but what's meant for you
will find it's way back to you
You can't fix people's fears
The hardest things to say
are sometimes the most important
Always tell the people you love you love them
Life isn't as serious as we make it out to be
Spend more time with your parents
They will leave sooner than you think
Death is not an ending
It's a beginning
Find comfort in silence
Read a book a week
Your biggest impact
is how you made people feel

So BE KIND
   BE PATIENT
   BE PRESENT

While you are still here

They ebb
and flow

THINGS I HAVE LEARNED THIS YEAR

Put yourself out there
Life's too short not to
Salt air is good for the heart
So swim in the ocean as much as possible
Love is complicated if you make it
But beautiful when you accept it
Make not a place but a community your home
People are more important than any destination
There's always a part of you
that will want what you don't have

And I think living is about finding a balance of contentment
The grass is always greener on the other side
For you have a better view

REALLY SEE

We fight the currents
Like its part of our being
We cannot go out with the tide
and rise in the evening
We are not able to
Light up the waters
When no one is watching

Why do we need an audience, always

I think life isn't about the moments of success
But of the in between
Uncertain
Sometimes mundane
Sometimes boring
Sitting with a pen in hand
Writing in the morning sunlight
I think living is but finding a flow
Of the life in front of you
Living through the moments you've been given
Not counting time
But appreciating a walk with friends
A homemade meal
Stargazing on our backs
Laughing till the moments passed
I think that is living
Not the planning ahead
But the being present
For all the little things we take for granted
Because life doesn't need to be a stadium stage
Life can be a backyard garden
Life can be watching the moon rise
in the afternoon haze
and the sun in the morning
Life is friends that hold you when your crying
Foreheads touching
Life isn't a grand production
of the success we may master
But the moments
People
Places
That got us to where we are going next

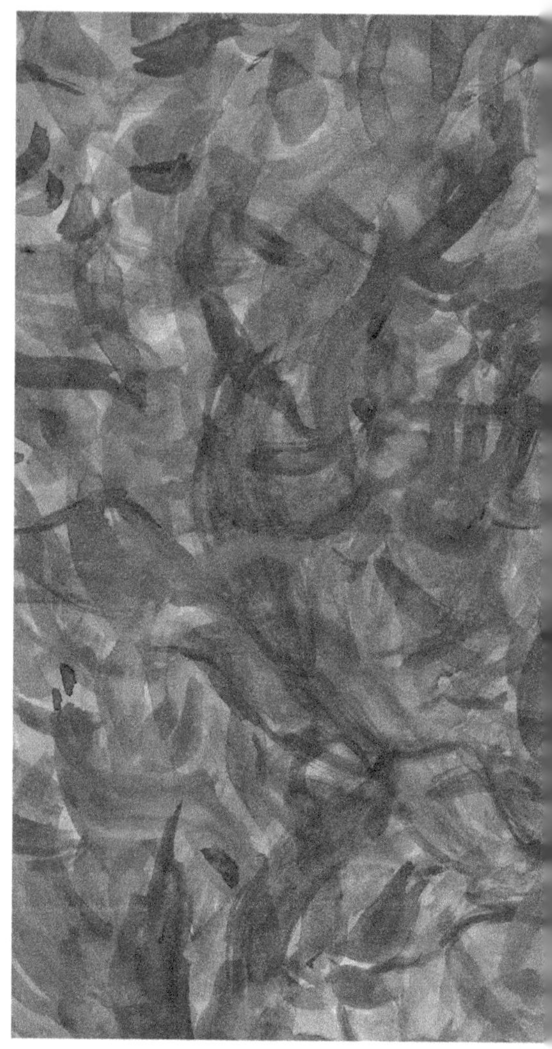

ACKNOWLEDGEMENTS

I would first like to thank the amazing team that made this book happen. My illustrator, editor, and all around talented human Nina Ripich for taking these poems and bringing them to life through illustrations. I cannot thank you enough for your dedication to this book. You dedicated your time, your talents, and your work to these pages and I am so grateful for you.

To Mira Horwitz, you see the world through such a beautiful lens and I am so thankful you let us share some of your film through these pages. Thank you for being such a supporter of *Remedies*. From coffee dates going over details, to helping plan a release schedule, you have been a steady hand to hold through it all. A big thanks to the Venice Photo Club and Curt Pittman as well for supporting this book and showcasing these poems through video and mixed media.

To my dad, you have been the biggest supporter of my art. I cannot thank you enough for pushing me to write every day. Your success with your own books and art inspired me to do the same and I am so happy that we get to share this love of words together. You have always pushed me to be my best self and to go after what I love. My favorite quote was one you told me years ago. You said "failure is the key to success", and I remember it every day.

A B O U T   A N N I

Anni is a gifted poet, singer/songwriter, and community leader. Her journey began with an innate love for both words and melodies. She found her artistic voice at a young age by writing poetry and studying piano, blending these passions to transform her verses into song lyrics. Her music became a channel for self-expression, capturing the essence of her experiences and emotions.

Anni started her first artist project under the name 'Annika Grace' in 2016. Since then, she has created a new artist project under the name 'Anni' exploring a more vulnerable, and raw side to her sound. You can listen to her music on all platforms.

She has been awarded First Place Gold Medalist for the World Poetry Movement's Best Poets and Poems and Gold Medalist in the International Who's Who in poetry contest. Her poetry has also won six silver keys in the Scholastic Art and Writing Awards.

In addition to her artistry, Anni has a strong commitment to community. Her love for music and her desire to foster creative connections inspired her to start the popular concert series, Saturdays at Seven. Starting as an intimate backyard gathering, this event has grown into a traveling showcase series in the Los Angeles area.

She currently lives and writes in Los Angeles, or can be found traveling along the California coast by sailboat, by train in Europe, or skiing the Rockies.

REMEDIES

Remedies

ISBN   979-8-8556-8727-9

Cover Design by Nina Ripich
Film by Mira Horwitz and Nina Ripich